TRYTHIS!
Gardening

Stephanie Turnbull

A+

Smart Apple Media

Designed and illustrated by Guy Callaby
Edited by Mary-Jane Wilkins

Cataloging-in-Publication Data is available from the Library of Congress

ISBN 978-1-62588-372-8

Photo acknowledgements
t = top, b = bottom, l = left, r = right, c = center
page 1 ChaiyonS021; 3 sanddebeautheil/both Shutterstock;
4 Anthony Harris/Thinkstock; 5tl Atelier_A, tr CBCK, br aarrows,
bl Luke Schmidt; 6l Grimplet, c Dionisvera, r photogal, b TAGSTOCK1/
all Shutterstock; 7, 9 Mim Waller; 10 Zerbor; 12 Peter Wey/both
Shutterstock; 13t Mim Waller, b toey19863; 14 Sergiy Bykhunenko;
16tr Soyka, tl V. J. Matthew, b Florin Burlan; 17 Sarycheva Olesia;
18 Madlen; 19 Igor Dutina; 20 Ellen Mol/all Shutterstock;
21 Mim Waller; 22l Bobkeenan Photography, r photoiconix;
23 Petr Malyshev/all Shutterstock
Cover top right Ryan McVay/Thinkstock; main image Pete Pahham/
Shutterstock

DAD0062
022015
9 8 7 6 5 4 3 2 1

Contents

Why try gardening?

Gardening is a fantastic hobby. Here are a few reasons to try it!

With just a little care and attention you can keep plants growing well and looking great all summer.

1 It's easy to do.

Planting seeds and watching them grow is something anyone can do. And if it goes wrong, just recycle your stuff in a **composter** and start again.

2 You don't need lots of space.

Having a huge garden is great, but you can grow all kinds of plants in pots or window boxes. Or how about keeping indoor plants on a windowsill?

3 It looks good...

Masses of colorful flowers can really brighten up your day— and they keep bees and other insects happy, too.

Remember to turn indoor pots as plants lean towards sunlight coming through the window.

4 ...and tastes great.

There's nothing like munching homegrown fruit, vegetables, and herbs!

Now test the brilliant projects in this book and see for yourself how much fun gardening can be. Look out for helpful tips and extra ideas.

No-soil growing

Start with this really simple growing idea— plants that don't need soil! You can do this indoors and you won't even get your hands dirty.

1 *Buy a few turnips, carrots, or parsnips.*

2 *Carefully chop off the tops with a knife, or ask an adult to do it.*

3 *Pour water into a saucer. Stand the vegetable tops in the water.*

4 *Leave in a bright, warm place and watch leaves shoot out in just a few days. Soon you'll have floating islands of greenery.*

Add more water every few days as the vegetables will soak it up.

Now try this

Push toothpicks into a sweet potato and balance it in a glass with water covering the lower part. In a few weeks roots will appear, followed by shoots on top of the potato. These can grow really tall!

Grass letters

Grass grows really quickly, so it's great for impatient gardeners—and good for creating arty designs.

1 *Find a **seed tray**. Fill it with a mixture of soil and **compost** from a bag. Rub the mixture between your hands to break up lumps.*

2 *With your finger or a stick, draw a letter in the soil. You could add a pattern or write your whole name if there's space!*

3 *Carefully sprinkle lots of grass seeds in the grooves. Use a funnel so seeds don't go all over the soil.*

4 *Sprinkle on more soil and compost to cover the seeds. Water them gently with a bottle spray.*

5 *Watch your letter appear over the next few weeks. Trim the grass with scissors to keep it neat.*

Water the tray regularly so the soil stays damp and the seeds grow.

Now try this

Secretly make a grass word or pattern for a friend, give them the tray, and tell them to water it.
As the grass grows, your surprise will be revealed!

Sweet mint syrup

**Mint is a herb that smells and tastes fantastic.
Grow your own and make yourself a sweet treat!**

1 *Buy a small mint plant and set it on a sunny windowsill, or outside on a patio.*

2 *Water it regularly and let it grow big and bushy. If flowers grow, pinch them off—they take the plant's energy away from growing leaves!*

3 *Pick a handful of leaves from the top of the plant and wash them well in a colander.*

4 Pour 10 fluid oz (250 ml) of water in a pan and add 4 oz (100g) sugar. Heat gently, stirring so the sugar **dissolves**.

5 Tear up the mint leaves and add them to the pan. Let the mixture boil and **simmer** for about ten minutes.

The pan will get hot, so ask an adult to help.

6 Leave to cool, then pour over ice cream.

Now try this

Make a refreshing minty drink by pouring boiling water over mint leaves, then **straining** the mixture into a glass. Stir in a little sugar, chill in the fridge and top up with fizzy water.

Rock gardens

Get creative and make a rock garden using small mountain plants called alpines. You can buy alpines at garden centers.

1 *Find a large pot with a hole in the bottom. The hole is important so that water can drain out. Alpines hate being soggy!*

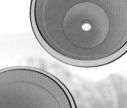

2 *Put some stones or bits of broken pot in the pot. This helps water run out easily.*

Many alpines grow close to the ground and produce masses of flowers.

3 Fill the pot with an equal mixture of soil and **grit**.

4 Arrange a few big stones on the top, then plant about three alpines around the stones.

5 Fill gaps around the plants with pebbles, then water the pot.

Plants spread as they grow, so don't plant them too close together.

These alpines have thick leaves that store water to keep the plants alive when it is very dry.

Now try this

Make a really colorful rock garden by using shiny gemstones instead of pebbles, or by adding extra decorations.

Easy seeds

Watching plants grow from seeds is great fun! Buy seeds that grow quickly, such as sunflowers or sweet peas.

1 *Fill a seed tray with equal amounts of compost and soil. Rub it between your hands to break up lumps.*

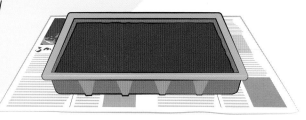

2 *Water the soil and scatter seeds evenly across it. Don't push them down. Sprinkle extra soil and compost on top.*

Seeds need to be near the surface, so add just enough soil to cover them.

3 Water the tray with a spray bottle and put it on a bright, warm windowsill. Cover with a clear plastic bag to keep moisture inside.

Some seed trays have clear plastic covers.

4 When **seedlings** sprout, remove the bag. As they grow, pinch out a few smaller ones to give the bigger ones more space.

5 When shoots have a few leaves, loosen the soil around them and gently take them out, without tearing the roots. Plant them in big pots or the garden.

Now try this

Decorate pots with **acrylic paints**, or glue on shells or plastic gems with craft glue. Use popsicle sticks as plant markers. Write the name of the plant on each stick, then push it into the soil.

Brilliant bulbs

Bulbs may look small and shriveled, but they produce thick, glossy leaves and beautiful flowers. Most need planting in autumn, then flower in spring.

1 *Dig over an area of soil in the garden and get rid of any weeds, or fill a big pot with soil and compost.*

Add grit, too—bulbs will rot if they're wet, and grit helps water drain out.

The pointy end is the top, where the stem will grow.

2 *Choose some bulbs, such as daffodils or tulips.*

The wider, flatter end is the base.

Wear gloves to handle them, as bulbs can irritate skin.

3 *Unlike seeds, most bulbs need burying deep. Make holes at least three times the height of the bulbs, push them in upright and cover them well.*

4 *Animals such as mice and squirrels love to nibble bulbs, so cover pots or flower beds with* **chicken wire**.

5 *Wait until spring and see green shoots push out of the soil!*

Chicken wire has sharp points, so ask an adult to help.

Now try this

Buy bulbs designed for growing indoors, such as amaryllis, which has huge, fantastic flowers. Cut off the flower stems when they die and let the leaves shrivel up. Next year they will all grow again!

Super spuds

You don't need lots of space to grow potatoes—an old sack will do! Buy **seed potatoes** and check what time of year to plant them.

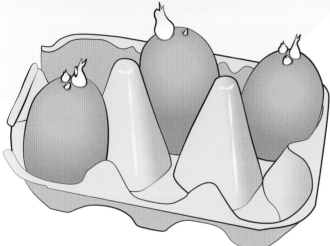

1 *Stand seed potatoes in an egg box. Leave them in a warm, sunny place for a few days until knobby sprouts appear. This is called chitting.*

2 *Find a large, empty compost or garbage bag and roll down the sides about a third of the way. Fill it with compost. Poke holes in the bottom so water can drain out.*

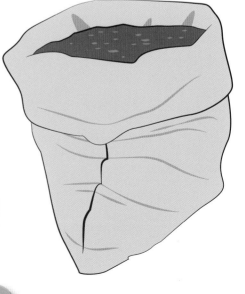

A full bag is heavy, so don't try to move it.

3 Space out a few potatoes on top of the soil. Cover them with about 4 inches (10 cm) of compost.

4 After a few weeks, leaves will sprout. Cover them with more compost. Water the soil regularly.

5 Keep covering leaves with compost, gradually unrolling the sides of the bag to make it taller. When the soil is nearly at the top of the bag, let the plants grow bushy.

6 When flowers appear, the potatoes should be ready. Carefully dig them up.

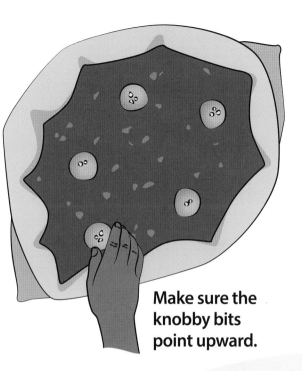

Make sure the knobby bits point upward.

Now try this

Scrub your freshly grown potatoes, prick holes with a fork and bake in the oven at 400°F (200°C) for about an hour. Split open and add cream cheese, tuna, ham, or grated cheese.

Miniature worlds

Use tiny plants, pebbles, toys, and plenty of imagination to create an amazing miniature garden!

1 Find a wide pot or a window box. Make sure it has holes in the bottom. Fill it with soil and compost.

*2 Choose a few small plants. Packs of four or six **plug plants** are just right. Look for short, tiny-leaved plants such as lobelia, alyssum, and thyme.*

3 Design your mini garden. You could have a winding path through the middle and a patio at the back. Plant your flowers, spacing them out.

4 *Add small, flat stones to make the patio and path. Fill gaps with pebbles or gravel.*

5 *Add extras such as toy chairs, fences from farm sets, or bottle lids for pots. A cocktail umbrella makes a good sunshade, and moss looks like grass.*

Now try this
Put toy figures in your miniature garden and take funny close-up photos.

Trim your plants to keep them tiny. If they grow too big, plant them in a real garden!

acrylic paints
Fast-drying paints that can be mixed with water or used straight from the tube. They won't wash off clothes when dry, so be careful.

chicken wire
A net of thin steel wires that can be bent into shapes, for example over the top of a flower pot.

chicken wire

compost
Rotted plants and other natural materials. Good compost is crumbly and dark.

composter
A metal, wooden, or plastic bin where dead plants and other garden waste rot and turn into compost.

dissolve
To gradually melt or mix in with a liquid, leaving no solid bits.

grit
Tiny bits of sand or stone.

plug plants
Tiny plants grown in a plastic container divided into separate compartments. Plug plants are often sold in packs of six, eight, or more. Carefully push out each seedling and plant it in a bigger pot, or in the ground.

plug plants

seedling
A tiny new plant, just starting to grow from a seed.

seed potatoes
A type of potato tuber (like a bulb) that has been specially grown to produce potatoes. Don't plant ordinary potatoes from the supermarket, as they may not grow a good crop.

seed tray
A wide, shallow container for planting seeds. Move seedlings into pots before they get too big, or the roots will tangle together and plants won't have space to grow properly.

simmer
To keep a liquid bubbling very gently at just under boiling point.

straining
Pouring a liquid through a mesh, such as a tea strainer, to separate out any solid bits.

strainer

Web sites

www.kidsgrowingstrong.org/flowers
Learn about flowers and how to grow them.

www.kiddiegardens.com
Discover all kinds of growing projects and garden crafts.

www.thecraftycrow.net/garden
Find ideas for brilliantly arty plant creations.